ADAPTATION FOR SURVIVAL

EYES

WRITTEN BY STEPHEN SAVAGE

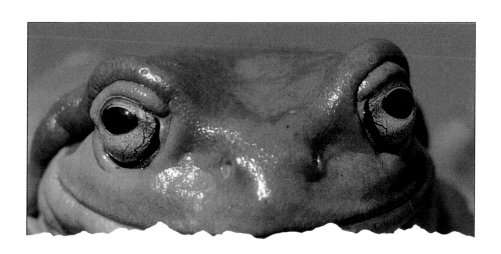

Thomson Learning
New York

ADAPTATION FOR SURVIVAL

Books in the series

• EARS • EYES • HANDS AND FEET
• MOUTHS • NOSES • SKIN

Front cover: An owl's eyes, a human's eyes and a cat's eyes.

Back cover: A human's eyes.

Title page: White's tree frog.

First published in the United States in 1995 by
Thomson Learning
115 Fifth Avenue
New York, NY 10003

Published simultaneously in Great Britain by Wayland (Publishers) Limited

U.S. version copyright © 1995 Thomson Learning

U.K. version copyright © 1995 Wayland (Publishers) Limited

Library of Congress Cataloging-in-Publication
Savage, Stephen.
    Eyes / Stephen Savage.
        p.   cm.—(Adaptation for survival)
    Includes bibliographical references and index.
    ISBN 1-56847-349-4
        1. Vision—Juvenile literature. 2. Eye—Juvenile literature.
    [1. Vision. 2. Eye.] I. Title. II. Series: Savage, Stephen, 1965–
    Adaptation for survival.
    QP475.7.S28   1995
    591.1'823—dc20   94-43226

Printed in Italy

Picture acknowledgments

The publishers would like to thank the following for allowing their photographs to be reproduced in this book: Bruce Coleman Ltd., 6 (below/Kim Taylor), 7 (left/Jane Burton), 9 (below/Hans Reinhard), 11 (above/Hans Reinhard), 11 (below/Kim Taylor), 12 (above/Paul Van Gaalen), 13 (Frank Greenaway), 15 (below/Rod Williams), 19 (above/Jane Burton), 20 (below/Bill Wood), 21 (Hans Reinhard), 24 (below/Kim Taylor), 25 (above/Jane Burton), 25 (below/P. Clement), 28 (above/Austin James Stevens), 29 (Jane Burton); Frank Lane Picture Agency 10 (above/Peter Davey); the Natural History Photographic Agency 8 (above/Nigel Dennis), 12 (below/Stephen Dalton), 15 (above/James Carmichael Jr., 17 (below/Daniel Heuclin), 19 (below/Daniel Heuclin), 27 (Jim Bain), 28 (below/B.G. Thomson); Oxford Scientific Films 8 (below/Mark Hamblin), 14 (Michael Leach), 16 (David Thompson), 17 (above/both Owen Newman), 18 (Darwin Dale), 20 (above/David B. Fleetham), 24 (above/J.A.L. Cooke), 26 (above/Alastair Macewen); Stephen Savage *title page;* Tony Stone Worldwide 5 (David Madison, *cover* (below) and 6 (above/Desmond Burdon), 7 (right/Ralph Wetmore), 10 (below/Purdy Matthews); Wayland *cover* (middle, spine and back); ZEFA front *cover* (top), 22 (below), 23.

Contents

The Human Eye

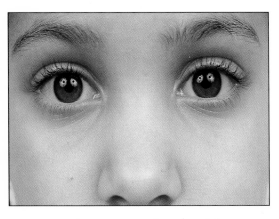

The colored part of the eye is called the iris, and the black hole in the center is the pupil.

Human eyes are similar in design to the eyes of most other mammals. Each eye sees a slightly different view from the other. The brain combines the two images to make the picture that we see.

If you look at an object in front of you, only the center of your view appears in sharp focus, while the edge of your vision is blurred. The clearest view is in the center where both images overlap. This type of vision is called binocular vision.

This is a simple diagram of a cross section through a human eye. See page 31 for more details of how we see.

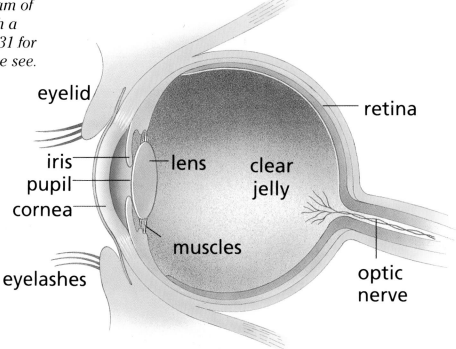

eyelid

retina

iris
pupil
cornea

lens

clear
jelly

muscles

eyelashes

optic
nerve

Binocular vision helps this tennis player to judge the direction, distance, and speed of the tennis ball. Binocular vision is just as important for judging distances in everyday actions such as picking up a glass of water.

Animals have eyes that are suited to their way of life. Some have eyes very similar to our own, but others have eyes that are very different. The world looks very much the same to a gorilla as it does to us. But the world looks very different to a bee. Some animals have better eyesight than we do, while other animals have very poor eyesight or none at all.

Seeing at Night

Many humans stay active after dark because of the artificial light created by electric lights. We do not have good night vision, but we can see in dim light. Some animals have excellent night vision and are only really active at night. These animals are called nocturnal. Their eyes are more sensitive than ours.

Some insects and small mammals feed at night when there are fewer dangers. Predators with night vision are able to find their prey in the darkness. Some animals, such as the domestic cat, leopard, and fox, are active day and night. At night, the pupil of each eye becomes bigger to allow more light in.

At night, this cat's pupils open to allow as much light as possible into the eye. The pupils close during the day to protect the eyes from bright sunlight. The pupils of human eyes open and close in the same way.

Many animals with night vision have a mirrorlike reflecting layer at the back of each eye. This gives the animal a much better chance of seeing even if there is only a smallest glimmer of light. This is why a cat's eyes appear to glow in the dark.

High in a tree, galagos run and leap in the branches looking for fruit and insects. A galago can leap to a nearby tree to escape danger.

Because their eyes are so large, most nocturnal animals cannot move their eyes the way we can. These animals must turn their heads to follow their prey. An owl can turn its head 180 degrees and actually see behind itself!

Looking Out for Danger

Meerkats are a kind of mongoose that live in groups underground. While members of the group look for food, one meerkat stands on its hind legs and keeps an eye out for danger.

Many animals need to keep a constant watch for danger. These animals have eyes on the sides of their heads, so they have a wide field of vision. Small birds have eyes that can focus on food in front of them. At the same time they can scan the surroundings for danger. Ducks and rabbits have eyes that have all-around vision, so they can even spot danger from behind.

When birds are feeding on the ground, they are easy prey. At the first sign of danger, feeding birds will take flight and settle on a nearby tree or rooftop.

Horses have eyes suited to life on the open plains. When feeding head down, they can focus on the grass and on any distant predators at the same time.

For most animals, the sight of a predator causes them to freeze or run away. A rabbit will often sit perfectly still, relying on its color to blend in with its surroundings. A squirrel will react by running up the nearest tree and climbing to the thin outer branches.

Squirrels have some binocular vision essential for judging distances when leaping from branch to branch. They cannot see directly behind them.

Looking for a Meal

Animals that hunt other animals for food usually have eyes on the fronts of their heads. This provides them with good binocular vision to judge the distance of their prey. Because they have eyes that face forward, these animals cannot see behind them. However, most of them are unlikely to be attacked from behind. Tigers, wolves, and foxes all have eyes in this position.

The clearest part of a predator's vision is in the center. The sharpest detail of a lion's vision is a horizontal strip. This helps the lion see its prey, which is often spread out in a herd on the horizon.

The beech marten's forward-facing eyes help it catch its prey.

▼ A chameleon can look in two directions at once.

Some predators, including wolves and lions, hunt in a group. Other predators, like the tiger, prefer to hunt alone.

Hunters come in all shapes and sizes. The chameleon is a tree-living lizard. It can move one eye at a time—one eye can look forward for its insect prey, while the other looks around for danger.

Human eyes are also on the front of the head. Although now most of us get our food from stores, our early ancestors were hunters.

From the Air

Eagles and hawks have excellent vision. They glide or hover high in the sky, scanning the ground for a potential meal. The center of their vision is magnified, which allows them to spot their prey from high up. This is similar to looking through a telescope.

Unlike most birds, eagles and hawks, such as this goshawk, have large eyes near the fronts of their heads. Binocular vision is the reason these birds are so successful at catching their prey.

The kestrel and sparrow hawk can hover over one place while searching for food. The kestrel's sight is so good that it can spot a mouse from a height of two hundred feet.

These hunting birds are called birds of prey. Most types feed on small mammals or other birds. When prey has been sighted, the bird swoops from the sky and grasps its prey in its talons. The osprey is sometimes called the fish hawk because it plunges into water to grasp a fish with its claws.

The beautiful kingfisher sits on a branch overlooking a stream. Once it spots a fish, it will plunge into the water to catch its meal.

Seabirds often catch fish by diving from the air. Pelicans dive into the sea and catch fish in their large throat pouches. When the common tern has spotted a fish, it dives into the sea, catching the fish in its long beak.

Third Eyelid

Like humans, many animals have eyelids to protect their eyes. Some animals also have eyelashes. When we blink our eyelids, salty tears wash across our eyes, keeping them clean and moist. The dirty tears drain from the eyes through tear ducts. A few mammals, such as the domestic cat, have the extra protection of a third eyelid, which is transparent.

The domestic cat is one of only a few mammals to have a third eyelid. Because they have this extra eyelid, cats blink fewer times than most other mammals (including humans).

Birds have a third eyelid, called a nictitating membrane, that moves sideways across the eyes and keeps them clean and moist. This means the bird does not have to blink and lose sight of its intended meal or a distant predator. A shark cannot close its normal eyelids, but some sharks have a third eyelid. This tough eyelid moves across the eye to protect it from attack while the shark is feeding.

▲ *Frogs can see underwater and on land with the help of a third eyelid. This tree frog can live out of water because its eyes are kept moist and clean.*

Crocodiles have a third eyelid similar to those of birds. This Nile crocodile's third eyelids help protect its eyes when underwater. ▶

Seeing with Invisible Light

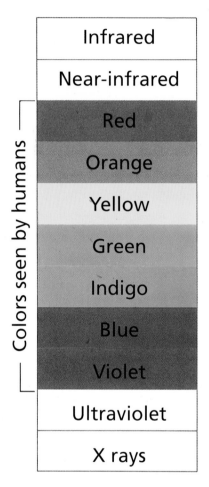

Infrared
Near-infrared
Red
Orange
Yellow
Green
Indigo
Blue
Violet
Ultraviolet
X rays

Colors seen by humans

Diagram to show the colors of light.

Bees use the position of the sun to find their way to and from their hive. They can even tell where the sun is on a cloudy day.

Like many mammals, humans have good vision. Sunlight is made up of various colors. These colors range from violet to red. Not all animals can see the same colors as we do, and so the world looks very different to them.

*Left: A flower as it would look to us. **Right:** A flower as it would look to a bee. Note the ultraviolet markings to attract insects.*

Although we cannot see ultraviolet light, there are animals that can. Our world of color looks very different to many insects, including bees. Some flowers have ultraviolet markings to attract insects. These markings lead the insect to the nectar and pollen at the center of the flower.

Some snakes have heat sense, which picks up the infrared body heat given off by mammals. The snake is able to see a heat picture of its intended prey. This heat sense is like having extra eyes. We have special cameras that can see heat pictures in the same way.

The heat-sensitive pits in front of this white-lipped pit viper's eyes will show the direction and distance of any warm objects. A snake's heat sense, the most sensitive known in the animal kingdom, allows these snakes to catch their prey in complete darkness.

Eyes within Eyes

Many small creatures, like insects and crabs, have two compound eyes. These large eyes are made up of thousands of tiny simple eyes that make one picture.

An insect has about 4,000 simple eyes in each of its two compound eyes. In this picture, each small dot is just one simple eye. These large compound eyes allow the insect to see all around it.

Some insects can see better than others. It depends on the number of simple eyes each compound eye is made of. The more simple the eye, the clearer the vision. Insects cannot see as clearly as humans can; their view is simple and fuzzy. However, compound eyes are very sensitive to movement.

▲ *The dragonfly has extremely good vision. Each compound eye has 30,000 simple eyes. The dragonfly's vision is so good that it can see and catch its flying insect prey in the air!*

◄ *A lobster's compound eyes are on stalks. Lobsters cannot move their heads like insects can. Instead, they can actually move their stalked eyes.*

Crabs, lobsters, and shrimps also have compound eyes. These eyes are good for spotting the movement of prey or a predator. If we had compound eyes, they would need to be three feet across to be as good as our own eyes!

Underwater Vision

The eyes of fish and other sea creatures are adapted to seeing underwater, but most fish cannot see above the water. However, the four-eyed fish is an exception and can look for food under the water and see any predators above the water at the same time.

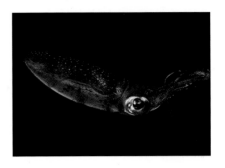

▲ Octopus and squid are very good hunters and have excellent eyesight. A close relative of this bigfin reef squid, the giant deep-sea squid has the largest eyes in the animal kingdom—they are the size of dinner plates!

Most fish have excellent color vision. This is why many fish are so beautifully colored. The colors of a fish's body are used to attract a mate, to advertise its territory, or to warn other animals that it is poisonous. Many fish can see in the dark depths of a pond or river. This is because they can see near-infrared light (see page 16) which is invisible to us.

◀ Coral reef fish are probably the most beautifully colored of all fish. If they are spotted by a predator, they can escape quickly by hiding in the branches of coral.

Sharks and their close relatives the rays probably cannot see in color. Their own bodies are not colorful. A shark's dark body color helps the shark to blend in with its surroundings.

Even a pet goldfish in a fish tank or garden pond can see near-infrared light. This helps the goldfish find food at the bottom of a dark, murky pond.

Seeing in Water and Air

A face mask allows this swimmer to see underwater. The air trapped behind the mask allows the swimmer's eyes to focus and see more clearly and prevents the salt water from stinging.

If you have ever swum in the sea without a face mask, you will realize how hard it is to see underwater. This is because our eyes are designed to work in air, so our vision underwater is blurred.

Dolphins have good vision below and above the water. Here, an inquisitive dolphin pokes its head above the water to look at its surroundings.

Like us, dolphins, whales, and seals are mammals. However, their eyes are adapted for seeing in air and in water. Seeing underwater has similar problems to seeing at night. Like nocturnal animals, the eyes of dolphins and seals have a mirror layer to reflect the small amount of light.

Dolphins, whales, and seals have special tear glands that produce an oily fluid that protects their eyes against the salty water. However, they do not have tear ducts like us, so the tears run down their faces. This is why seals on land have wet patches around their eyes as if they have been crying.

Seals have very large eyes that are good for hunting fish in gloomy water. Their vision underwater is better than it is on land.

Eye Changes

The eyes of a few animals change during their lives as they develop from a young animal to an adult. The larvae of some insects—caterpillars, for example—have only simple eyes. By the time the caterpillar has become a butterfly it has two large compound eyes.

A caterpillar does not need complex eyes to find food. The butterfly lays its eggs on plants that the newly hatched caterpillar will eat. When it becomes a butterfly, it needs complex eyes for flying and finding food.

When a frog tadpole hatches from its egg, it is born into a world of water. The tiny tadpole swims around its pond feeding on plants and small creatures. As the tadpole develops into a frog, its eyes change so that the adult frog will be able to see on land.

A flatfish starts off life swimming upright like any other fish. The baby flatfish has an eye on each side of its head. As it grows, one eye slowly moves across the head so both eyes are on one side. This side becomes the top and the flatfish swims on its side.

Adult frogs can see on land and underwater. Their eyes are on the top of their heads and point slightly forward. The frog's eyes are very sensitive to movement, which helps it to catch its prey.

Many Eyes

Some animals have more than just two eyes, and some insects have two types of eye. Dragonflies and wasps have two compound eyes, but they also have simple eyes. The simple eyes of a dragonfly can only detect light and help it to fly level by detecting the light from the sky.

As well as having compound eyes, this wasp also has simple eyes.

Hunting spiders have very good vision for hunting other small creatures. The simple eyes look for movement, so they are good for detecting prey or danger.

Some spiders have six or even eight eyes. Each of these spiders has two large eyes at the front for seeing its prey. It also has several simple eyes on each side of its head for seeing movement. These simple eyes will help warn the spider of any danger.

The scallop has two halves to its shell and lives on the seabed. It has two rows of eyes around its shell and may have as many as forty eyes in total. The scallop's many eyes are well placed for spotting danger. When there is danger, the scallop shuts its shell tightly.

If a predator such as a starfish approaches, the scallop can escape by "swimming." The scallop does this by rapidly opening and closing its shell.

No Eyes

The snail has light-sensitive eyes at the end of its tentacles. Snails avoid the sunlight and are active mainly at night.

The type of vision an animal has not only depends on its eyes but also on its brain. Mammals have large brains so they have very detailed vision. Some creatures have eyes that can only see light and dark. Snails cannot see a detailed image and can only detect the direction of light. However, this is very useful to the snail, because it would soon dry out and die in sunlight.

Earthworms do not need eyes. They live underground, feeding on decaying plant matter. They move through hard soil by eating their way through it. Earthworms only come to the surface at night or when it rains.

A few types of mammals have eyes but they cannot see. The marsupial mole lives in underground burrows and has no need of sight.

Some animals have no eyes at all. The blind mole rat lives underground and finds its way around by using sensitive whiskers at both ends of its body. A sea anemone stings prey and enemies alike by reacting to touch. Animals such as these can find food, avoid danger, or find a mate by using their other senses.

Having no eyes, the sea anemone has to rely on small sea creatures swimming into its tentacles. The anemone then stings and eats the creatures.

Glossary

Binocular vision Vision that blends the sight from two eyes to form a single image, which is clearest in the center. Humans have binocular vision.

Color spectrum Colors that make up white light.

Compound eyes Large eyes made up of hundreds of small eyes. Insects, crabs, and lobsters all have these kinds of eyes.

Infrared light A type of red light at the red end of the color spectrum that is invisible to humans but can be seen by some animals. Warm animals give off infrared body heat that can be seen by a few animals.

Near-infrared light A type of red light at the red end of the color spectrum that is invisible to humans but can be seen by some animals such as goldfish.

Nocturnal An animal that is active at night.

Predator An animal that kills other animals for food.

Simple eyes Eyes that can only see light, dark, and movement, but not colors or details.

Telescope An optical instrument that makes distant objects appear closer.

Ultraviolet A type of violet light at the violet end of the color spectrum which is invisible to humans but can be seen by some animals. Ultraviolet rays from the sun can cause sunburn.

Further Reading

Bennett, Paul. *Catching a Meal.* Nature's Secrets. New York: Thomson Learning, 1994.

Parker, Steve. *The Eye and Seeing* . The Human Body. Revised edition. New York: Franklin Watts, 1989.

Sinclair, Sandra. *Extraordinary Eyes: How Animals See.* New York: Dial Books Young Readers, 1992.

Further Notes

Humans have five senses, each of which contributes to our awareness of our environment, therefore helping us to survive. All animals view the world through a combination of senses. Their senses collect information that is relevant to their survival, so many animals perceive the world differently from humans.

Parts of the human eye

Iris - Colored part around the pupil

Cornea - Protects the lens and helps focus light

Lens - Focuses light from an object

Pupil - Opens and closes to allow light into eye

Retina - Light-sensitive area of eye

Optic nerve - Carries image to brain

Eyelids - Protect eye

Eyelashes - Protect eye from dust and dirt

Eye muscles - Move eyeball

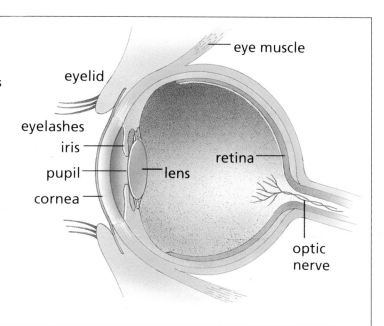

How we see

Light from an object passes through the **pupil** and is focused by the **lens** to make a tiny upside-down picture on the **retina** at the back of the eye. The image is then carried along the **optic nerve** to the brain where the picture is turned the right way up. The brain also interprets what is seen. This interpretation is often based on knowledge and experience.

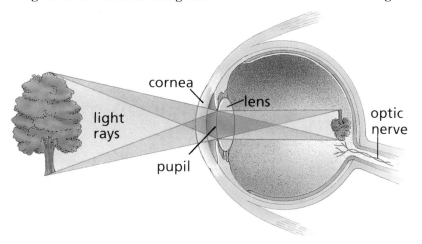

Index